Gooseberry Patch
2500 Farmers Dr., #110
Columbus, OH 43235

www.gooseberrypatch.com
1·800·854·6673

Your recipe could appear in our next cookbook!

Share your tried & true family favorite recipes with us instantly at

www.gooseberrypatch.com

If you'd rather jot 'em down by hand, send them to us at:
Gooseberry Patch
Attn: Cookbook Dept.
2500 Farmers Dr., #110
Columbus, OH 43235

Don't forget to include the number of servings your recipe makes,
plus your name, address, phone number and email address. If we select
your recipe, your name will appear right along with it
and you'll receive a **FREE** copy of the cookbook!

January

January

Notes

Sunday	Monday	Tuesday
A house that does not have one worn, comfy chair in it is soulless. *— May Sarton*		**1** New Year's Day
6	**7**	**8**
13	**14**	**15**
20	**21** **Martin Luther King, Jr. Day**	**22**
27	**28**	**29**

December

S	M	T	W	T	F	S
						1
2	3	4	5	6	7	8
9	10	11	12	13	14	15
16	17	18	19	20	21	22
23	24	25	26	27	28	29
30	31					

February

S	M	T	W	T	F	S
					1	2
3	4	5	6	7	8	9
10	11	12	13	14	15	16
17	18	19	20	21	22	23
24	25	26	27	28		

2013

Wednesday	Thursday	Friday	Saturday
2	3	4	5
9	10	11	12
16	17	18	19
23 / 30	24 / 31	25	26

Combat the winter doldrums...create a deliciously citrus-scented centerpiece! Pierce small holes in limes, lemons and oranges using a toothpick, then fill each hole with a whole clove. Place fruit in a bowl for a fresh-smelling centerpiece that's sure to brighten any day.

January

1 Tuesday   New Year's Day

2 Wednesday

3 Thursday

4 Friday

5 Saturday

6 Sunday

January

Monday 7

Tuesday 8

Wednesday 9

Thursday 10

Friday 11

Saturday 12

Sunday 13

January

14 Monday

15 Tuesday

16 Wednesday

17 Thursday

18 Friday

19 Saturday

20 Sunday

January

**Martin Luther
King, Jr. Day**

Monday 21

Tuesday 22

Wednesday 23

Thursday 24

Friday 25

Saturday 26

Sunday 27

January

28 Monday

29 Tuesday

30 Wednesday

31 Thursday

Pull-Apart Pizza Bread

12-oz. tube refrigerated
   flaky biscuits, quartered
1 T. olive oil
12 slices pepperoni,
   quartered
1/4 c. shredded mozzarella
   cheese

1 onion, chopped
1 t. Italian seasoning
1/4 t. garlic salt
1/4 c. grated Parmesan
   cheese

Brush biscuits with oil; set aside. Combine
remaining ingredients in a bowl; add
biscuits. Toss well; arrange in a Bundt®
pan lined with well-greased aluminum
foil. Bake at 400 degrees for 15 minutes.
Pull bread apart to serve. Makes about 2 dozen pieces.

February

February

Sunday   Monday   Tuesday

Too much of a good thing is wonderful.

—Mae West

Sunday	Monday	Tuesday
3	4	5
10	11	12 **Lincoln's Birthday**
17	18 **Presidents' Day**	19
24	25	26

January

S	M	T	W	T	F	S
		1	2	3	4	5
6	7	8	9	10	11	12
13	14	15	16	17	18	19
20	21	22	23	24	25	26
27	28	29	30	31		

March

S	M	T	W	T	F	S
					1	2
3	4	5	6	7	8	9
10	11	12	13	14	15	16
17	18	19	20	21	22	23
24	25	26	27	28	29	30
31						

2013

Wednesday	Thursday	Friday	Saturday
		1	2 **Groundhog Day**
6	7	8	9
13 **Ash Wednesday**	14 **Valentine's Day**	15	16
20	21	22 **Washington's Birthday**	23
27	28		

February

Iced Raspberry Delights

16-1/2 oz. tube refrigerated
    sugar cookie dough
1-1/4 c. white chocolate
    chunks, divided

12-oz. jar seedless
    raspberry jam
1 t. oil

Press dough into an ungreased 13"x9" baking pan.
Evenly press one cup chocolate chunks into dough. Bake
at 350 degrees for 16 to 20 minutes, until lightly golden.
Spread jam over crust; bake an additional 10 minutes. Cool
completely. Cut into squares or use a cookie cutter to cut into
shapes. Combine remaining chocolate and oil in a plastic
zipping bag. Microwave 30 to 45 seconds; squeeze bag until
chocolate is melted. Snip off tip of one corner and
drizzle over bars. Refrigerate until set.
Makes 3 dozen.

1 Friday

2 Saturday   **Groundhog Day**

3 Sunday

February

Monday 4

Tuesday 5

Wednesday 6

Thursday 7

Friday 8

Saturday 9

Sunday 10

February

11 Monday

12 Tuesday   **Lincoln's Birthday**

13 Wednesday   **Ash Wednesday**

14 Thursday   **Valentine's Day**

15 Friday

16 Saturday

17 Sunday

February

Monday **18**

Tuesday **19**

Wednesday **20**

Thursday **21**

Friday **22**

Saturday **23**

Sunday **24**

February

25 Monday

26 Tuesday

27 Wednesday

28 Thursday

Cookie swaps aren't just for Christmas...how about hosting a Valentine's Day cookie swap? Invite 6 to 8 friends and ask them to bring 1/2 dozen cookies for each guest. They'll go home with as many as they brought...unless the munching begins at the party!

March

March

Notes

Sunday   Monday   Tuesday

3	4	5
10 **Daylight Savings Begins**	11 **Commonwealth Day (Canada)**	12
17 **St. Patrick's Day**	18	19
24 **Palm Sunday** / 31 **Easter**	25 **Passover**	26

February
S	M	T	W	T	F	S
					1	2
3	4	5	6	7	8	9
10	11	12	13	14	15	16
17	18	19	20	21	22	23
24	25	26	27	28		

April
S	M	T	W	T	F	S
	1	2	3	4	5	6
7	8	9	10	11	12	13
14	15	16	17	18	19	20
21	22	23	24	25	26	27
28	29	30				

2013

Wednesday	Thursday	Friday	Saturday
May the roof above us never fall in, and may we friends gathered here never fall out. *– Irish blessing*		1	2
6	7	8	9
13	14	15	16
20 **First Day of Spring**	21	22	23
27	28	29 **Good Friday**	30

March

Grandma's Potato Soup

2 lbs. potatoes, peeled and
    diced
1/2 lb. carrots, peeled and
    diced
2 stalks celery, diced
1 onion, diced
4 c. water
12-oz. can evaporated milk

1/4 c. butter, sliced
onion and garlic seasoned
    salt to taste
pepper to taste
8-oz. pkg. shredded
    Cheddar cheese
3 slices bacon, crisply
    cooked and crumbled

Combine vegetables and water in a stockpot over
medium-high heat. Cook until vegetables are fork-tender,
15 to 20 minutes. Reduce heat to low; stir in evaporated
milk, butter and seasonings. Heat through. Ladle into soup
bowls; garnish with cheese and bacon. Serves 6.

1   Friday

2   Saturday

3   Sunday

March

Monday 4

Tuesday 5

Wednesday 6

Thursday 7

Friday 8

Saturday 9

Daylight Savings Begins

Sunday 10

March

11 Monday   **Commonwealth Day (Canada)**

12 Tuesday

13 Wednesday

14 Thursday

15 Friday

16 Saturday

17 Sunday   **St. Patrick's Day**

March

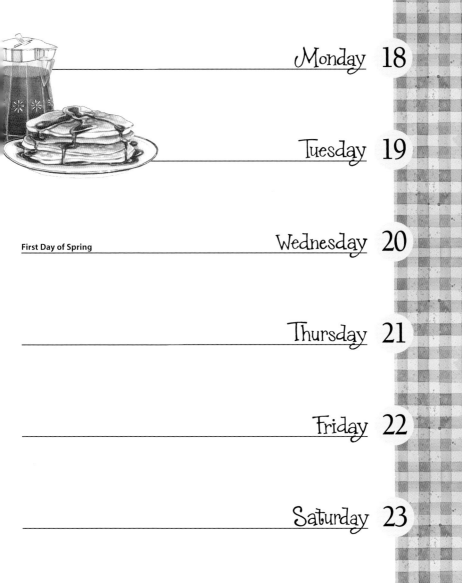

Monday 18

Tuesday 19

First Day of Spring   Wednesday 20

Thursday 21

Friday 22

Saturday 23

Palm Sunday   Sunday 24

March

25 Monday Passover

26 Tuesday

27 Wednesday

28 Thursday

29 Friday Good Friday

30 Saturday

31 Sunday Easter

April

Sunday	Monday	Tuesday
	1 **April Fool's Day** **Easter Monday** **(Canada)**	2
7	8	9
14	15	16
21	22	23
28	29	30

March

S	M	T	W	T	F	S
					1	2
3	4	5	6	7	8	9
10	11	12	13	14	15	16
17	18	19	20	21	22	23
24	25	26	27	28	29	30
31						

May

S	M	T	W	T	F	S
			1	2	3	4
5	6	7	8	9	10	11
12	13	14	15	16	17	18
19	20	21	22	23	24	25
26	27	28	29	30	31	

2013

Wednesday	Thursday	Friday	Saturday
3	4	5	6
10	11	12	13
17	19	19	20
24	25	26	27

I had rather be on my farm than
be emperor of the world.
— *George Washington*

April

1 Monday _____ **April Fool's Day**
Easter Monday (Canada)

2 Tuesday _____

3 Wednesday _____

4 Thursday _____

5 Friday _____

6 Saturday _____

7 Sunday _____

April

Wednesday 10

Thursday 11

Friday 12

Saturday 13

Sunday 14

April

15 Monday _____

16 Tuesday _____

17 Wednesday _____

18 Thursday _____

19 Friday _____

20 Saturday _____

21 Sunday _____

April

Monday 22

Tuesday 23

Wednesday 24

Thursday 25

Friday 26

Saturday 27

Sunday 28

April

Morning Mix-Up

2 c. frozen diced potatoes
1 c. cooked ham, chopped
1/2 c. onion, chopped
2 T. oil
6 eggs, beaten

salt and pepper to taste
1 c. shredded Cheddar
  cheese

In a large skillet over medium heat, sauté potatoes, ham and onion in oil for 10 minutes, or until potatoes are tender. Whisk eggs with salt and pepper. Reduce heat to low; add eggs to skillet. Cook, stirring occasionally, until eggs are set. Remove from heat and gently stir in cheese. Serves 4.

friends

May

May

Sunday   Monday   Tuesday

If more of us valued food and cheer and song above hoarded gold, it would be a merrier world.

— *J. R. R. Tolkien*

Sunday	Monday	Tuesday
5	6	7
12	13	14
	Mothers' Day	
19	20	21
	Victoria Day (Canada)	
26	27	28
	Memorial Day	

April
S	M	T	W	T	F	S
	1	2	3	4	5	6
7	8	9	10	11	12	13
14	15	16	17	18	19	20
21	22	23	24	25	26	27
28	29	30				

June
S	M	T	W	T	F	S
						1
2	3	4	5	6	7	8
9	10	11	12	13	14	15
16	17	18	19	20	21	22
23	24	25	26	27	28	29
30						

2013

Wednesday	Thursday	Friday	Saturday
1 **May Day**	2	3	4
8	9	10	11
15	16	17	18
22	23	24	25
29	30	31	

May

Fresh Guacamole

6 avocados, halved and
 pitted
3 T. lime juice
1/2 yellow onion, finely
 chopped
4 roma tomatoes, chopped
3/4 c. sour cream

1 T. ranch salad dressing
1 T. salt, or to taste
1 T. pepper, or to taste
1 T. chili powder
1/2 t. cayenne pepper
Garnish: fresh cilantro sprigs
tortilla chips

Scoop out avocado pulp into a large bowl; mash with a fork.
Add lime juice, onion and tomatoes; mix with a spoon. Add
sour cream, salad dressing and seasonings; mix well. Cover
with plastic wrap; refrigerate for at least 30 minutes. Garnish
with cilantro. Serve with tortilla chips. Makes 8 to 10 servings.

1 Wednesday _____ **May Day**

2 Thursday _____

3 Friday _____

4 Saturday _____

5 Sunday _____

May

Monday 6

Tuesday 7

Wednesday 8

Thursday 9

Friday 10

Saturday 11

Mothers' Day   Sunday 12

May

13 Monday _____

14 Tuesday _____

15 Wednesday _____

16 Thursday _____

17 Friday _____

18 Saturday _____

19 Sunday _____

May

Monday **20**

Tuesday **21**

Wednesday **22**

Thursday **23**

Friday **24**

Saturday **25**

Sunday **26**

May

27 Monday   **Memorial Day**

28 Tuesday

29 Wednesday

30 Thursday

31 Friday

Say it with Flowers:

Acacia...Secret Love

Camellia...Excellence

Carnation...Distinction

Forget-me-not...True love

Daisy...Innocence

Gardenia...Joy

Honeysuckle...Devotion

Ivy...Marriage, Fidelity

Lily...Purity

Lily-of-the-Valley...Happiness

Orange Blossom...Loveliness & Happiness

Rosemary...Remembrance

Pansy...Shyness

Rose...Love

June

June

Notes

Sunday   Monday   Tuesday

2	3	4
9	10	11
16	17	18
	Fathers' Day	
23 / 30	24	25

May
S M T W T F S
              1 2 3 4
 5 6 7 8 9 10 11
12 13 14 15 16 17 18
19 20 21 22 23 24 25
26 27 28 29 30 31

July
S M T W T F S
    1 2 3 4 5 6
 7 8 9 10 11 12 13
14 15 16 17 18 19 20
21 22 23 24 25 26 27
28 29 30 31

2013

Wednesday	Thursday	Friday	Saturday
In the morning, very early, that's the time I love to go barefoot where the fern grows curly and grass is cool between each toe. On a summer morning-O! On a summer morning. — Rachel Field			1
5	6	7	8
12	13	14 **Flag Day**	15
19	20	21 **First Day of Summer**	22
26	27	28	29

June

Bacon-Stuffed Burgers

4 slices bacon, crisply
   cooked, crumbled and
   drippings reserved
1/4 c. onion, chopped
4-oz. can mushroom pieces,
   drained and diced
1 lb. ground beef
1 lb. ground pork sausage

1/4 c. grated Parmesan
   cheese
1/2 t. pepper
1/2 t. garlic powder
2 T. steak sauce
8 sandwich buns, split
Optional: lettuce

Heat 2 tablespoons reserved drippings in a skillet over
medium heat. Add onion and sauté until tender. Add bacon
and mushrooms; heat through and set aside. Combine beef,
sausage, pepper, garlic powder and steak sauce in a large
bowl. Shape into 16 thin patties. Spoon bacon mixture over
8 patties. Place remaining patties on top
and press edges tightly to seal. Grill
over medium coals to desired
doneness. Serve on buns
with lettuce, if desired.
Makes 8 servings.

1 Saturday

2 Sunday

June

Monday **3**

_____

Tuesday **4**

_____

Wednesday **5**

_____

Thursday **6**

_____

Friday **7**

_____

Saturday **8**

_____

Sunday **9**

_____

June

10 Monday

11 Tuesday

12 Wednesday

13 Thursday

14 Friday   Flag Day

15 Saturday

16 Sunday   Fathers' Day

June

Monday 17

Tuesday 18

Wednesday 19

Thursday 20

First Day of Summer   Friday 21

Saturday 22

Sunday 23

June

24 Monday

25 Tuesday

26 Wednesday

27 Thursday

28 Friday

29 Saturday

30 Sunday

July

July

Sunday	Monday	Tuesday
	1 **Canada Day (Canada)**	2
7	8	9
14	15	16
21	22	23
28	29	30

June

S	M	T	W	T	F	S
						1
2	3	4	5	6	7	8
9	10	11	12	13	14	15
16	17	18	19	20	21	22
23	24	25	26	27	28	29
30						

August

S	M	T	W	T	F	S
				1	2	3
4	5	6	7	8	9	10
11	12	13	14	15	16	17
18	19	20	21	22	23	24
25	26	27	28	29	30	31

2013

Wednesday	Thursday	Friday	Saturday
3	4 **Independence Day**	5	6
10	11	12	13
17	18	19	20
24	25	26	27
31			

It's difficult to think anything but pleasant thoughts while eating a homegrown tomato.

— *Lewis Grizzard*

July

1 Monday   Canada Day (Canada)

2 Tuesday

3 Wednesday

4 Thursday   Independence Day

5 Friday

6 Saturday

7 Sunday

July

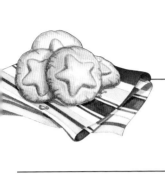

Monday 8

Tuesday 9

Wednesday 10

Thursday 11

Friday 12

Saturday 13

Sunday 14

July

15 _Monday_

16 _Tuesday_

17 _Wednesday_

18 _Thursday_

19 _Friday_

20 _Saturday_

21 _Sunday_

July

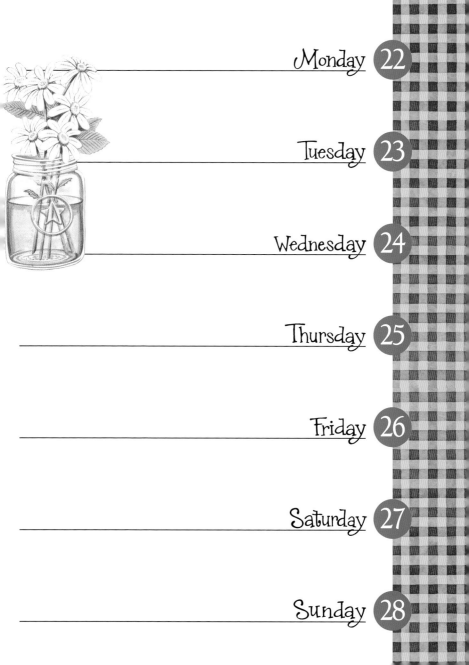

Monday 22

Tuesday 23

Wednesday 24

Thursday 25

Friday 26

Saturday 27

Sunday 28

July

29 *Monday*

30 *Tuesday*

31 *Wednesday*

Summertime Tomato Tart

4 tomatoes, sliced
9-inch pie crust
8-oz. pkg. shredded
   mozzarella cheese

2 T. fresh basil, chopped
1/4 c. olive oil

Arrange tomato slices in bottom of pie crust. Sprinkle evenly with cheese and basil; drizzle with oil. Bake at 400 degrees for 30 minutes. Let stand for 5 minutes before slicing. Serves 6.

August

August

Sunday   Monday   Tuesday

Food for thought is no substitute
for the real thing.

– Walt Kelly

Sunday	Monday	Tuesday
4	5	6
11	12	13
18	19	20
25	26	27

July

S	M	T	W	T	F	S
	1	2	3	4	5	6
7	8	9	10	11	12	13
14	15	16	17	18	19	20
21	22	23	24	25	26	27
28	29	30	31			

September

S	M	T	W	T	F	S
1	2	3	4	5	6	7
8	9	10	11	12	13	14
15	16	17	18	19	20	21
22	23	24	25	26	27	28
29	30					

2013

Wednesday	Thursday	Friday	Saturday
	1	2	3
7	8	9	10
14	15	16	17
21	22	23	24
28	29	30	31

August

Spiced Zucchini Bars

2 c. all-purpose flour
2 t. baking soda
1/2 t. salt
2 t. cinnamon
3 eggs, beaten
1 c. oil

2 c. sugar
1 t. vanilla extract
1 t. lemon juice
1 c. raisins
2 c. zucchini, grated
3/4 c. chopped nuts

Zucchini

Combine dry ingredients in a small bowl; set aside. In a separate bowl, whisk together eggs, oil, sugar, vanilla and lemon juice. Gradually add flour mixture to egg mixture. Fold in remaining ingredients; pour into a greased and floured 15"x10" jelly-roll pan. Bake at 325 degrees for 25 to 35 minutes, until lightly golden. Cool; cut into bars. Makes 3 dozen.

1 Thursday

2 Friday

3 Saturday

4 Sunday

August

Monday **5**

Tuesday **6**

Wednesday **7**

Thursday **8**

Friday **9**

Saturday **10**

Sunday **11**

August

12 Monday
_____

13 Tuesday
_____

14 Wednesday
_____

15 Thursday
_____

16 Friday
_____

17 Saturday
_____

18 Sunday
_____

August

Monday 19

Tuesday 20

Wednesday 21

Thursday 22

Friday 23

Saturday 24

Sunday 25

August

26 Monday _____

27 Tuesday _____

28 Wednesday _____

29 Thursday _____

30 Friday _____

31 Saturday _____

September

September

Notes

Sunday	Monday	Tuesday
1	2 **Labor Day**	3
8 **Grandparents' Day**	9	10
15	16	17
22 **First Day of Autumn**	23	24
29	30	

August

S	M	T	W	T	F	S
				1	2	3
4	5	6	7	8	9	10
11	12	13	14	15	16	17
18	19	20	21	22	23	24
25	26	27	28	29	30	31

October

S	M	T	W	T	F	S
		1	2	3	4	5
6	7	8	9	10	11	12
13	14	15	16	17	18	19
20	21	22	23	24	25	26
27	28	29	30	31		

2013

Wednesday	Thursday	Friday	Saturday
4 **Rosh Hashanah**	5	6	7
11 **Patriot Day**	12	13 **Yom Kippur**	14
18	19	20	21
25	26	27	28

After dinner sit a while, and after supper walk a mile.

– English Saying

September

Autumn Apple Milkshake

14-oz. can sweetened
   condensed milk
1 c. applesauce
1/2 c. apple cider

1/2 t. apple pie spice
3 c. crushed ice
Garnish: cinnamon

In a blender, combine all ingredients except ice and
cinnamon. Gradually add ice, blending until smooth. Garnish
with cinnamon. Serves 4 to 6.

1 Sunday

September

Labor Day   *Monday* 2

                                                        Tuesday 3

Rosh Hashanah   *Wednesday* 4

                                                      Thursday 5

                                                        Friday 6

                                                      Saturday 7

Grandparents' Day   *Sunday* 8

September

9 Monday

10 Tuesday

11 Wednesday   **Patriot Day**

12 Thursday

13 Friday   **Yom Kippur**

14 Saturday

15 Sunday

September

Monday 16

Tuesday 17

Wednesday 18

Thursday 19

Friday 20

Saturday 21

First Day of Autumn Sunday 22

September

23 Monday

24 Tuesday

25 Wednesday

26 Thursday

27 Friday

28 Saturday

29 Sunday

September

Keep a warm quilt or blanket-stitched throw
in the car for autumn picnics and football
games...perfect for keeping warm & cozy!

Hot Buffalo Dip

3 to 4 boneless, skinless
    chicken breasts, cooked
    and chopped
1 c. hot wing sauce
2 8-oz. pkgs. cream cheese,
    softened and cubed

1/2 c. shredded Cheddar
    cheese
1/4 c. blue cheese salad
    dressing
corn chips, celery stalks

In a slow cooker, mix together all ingredients except crackers or tortillas. Cover and cook on high setting for 5 hours. Serve with corn chips and celery stalks for dipping. Serves 8 to 10.

Ripe Tomatoes

Bi-Color Sweet Corn

SQUASH

on

October

October

Sunday	Monday	Tuesday
Autumn is a second spring when every leaf is a flower. – Albert Camus		1
6	7	8
13	14 **Columbus Day Thanksgiving (Canada)**	15
20	21	22
27	28	29

September

S	M	T	W	T	F	S
1	2	3	4	5	6	7
8	9	10	11	12	13	14
15	16	17	18	19	20	21
22	23	24	25	26	27	28
29	30					

November

S	M	T	W	T	F	S
					1	2
3	4	5	6	7	8	9
10	11	12	13	14	15	16
17	18	19	20	21	22	23
24	25	26	27	28	29	30

2013

Wednesday	Thursday	Friday	Saturday
2	3	4	5
9	10	11	12
16	17	18	19 **Sweetest Day**
23	24	25	26
30	31 **Halloween**		

October

Field pumpkins, which are bred for perfect jack-o'-lanterns, tend to be too large and stringy for baking. Look for sugar pumpkins instead...a medium-sized sugar pumpkin will yield about 1-1/2 cups of mashed pumpkin. This purée can be used in all your recipes calling for canned pumpkin.

1 Tuesday

2 Wednesday

3 Thursday

4 Friday

5 Saturday

6 Sunday

October

Monday 7

Tuesday 8

Wednesday 9

Thursday 10

Friday 11

Saturday 12

Sunday 13

October

14 Monday

Columbus Day
Thanksgiving (Canada)

15 Tuesday

16 Wednesday

17 Thursday

18 Friday

19 Saturday

Sweetest Day

20 Sunday

October

Monday 21

Tuesday 22

Wednesday 23

Thursday 24

Friday 25

Saturday 26

Sunday 27

October

28 Monday

29 Tuesday

30 Wednesday

31 Thursday   Halloween

Chocolate Chippy Pumpkin Bread

3 c. all-purpose flour
1 t. baking soda
1 t. salt
2 t. cinnamon
4 eggs

2 c. sugar
15-oz. can pumpkin
1-1/4 c. oil
1-1/2 c. semi-sweet
    chocolate chips

Combine flour, baking soda, salt and cinnamon in a large
bowl; set aside. Beat together eggs, sugar, pumpkin and oil
in a large bowl; stir into dry ingredients just until moistened.
Fold in chocolate chips; pour into 2 greased 8"x4" loaf pans.
Bake at 350 degrees for 60 to 70 minutes, until a toothpick
tests clean. Cool for 10 minutes before removing to wire
racks to finish cooling. Makes 2 loaves.

November

November

Notes

Serve hot spiced coffee with sweet autumn treats. Simply add 3/4 teaspoon pumpkin pie spice to 1/2 cup ground coffee and brew as usual.

Sunday	Monday	Tuesday
3 **Daylight Savings Ends**	4	5 **Election Day**
10	11 **Veterans' Day** **Remembrance Day** **(Canada)**	12
17	18	19
24	25	26

2013

Wednesday	Thursday	Friday	Saturday
		1	2
6	7	8	9
13	14	15	16
20	21	22	23
27 Hanukkah	28 Thanksgiving	29	30

November

Homemade Turkey Pot Pie

1/3 c. margarine
1/3 c. onion, chopped
1/3 c. all-purpose flour
1/2 t. salt
1/4 t. pepper
1-3/4 c. turkey broth

2/3 c. milk
2-1/2 to 3 c. cooked turkey, chopped
10-oz. pkg. frozen peas and carrots, thawed
2 9-inch pie crusts

Melt margarine in a large saucepan over low heat. Stir in onion, flour, salt and pepper. Cook, stirring constantly, until mixture is bubbly; remove from heat. Stir in broth and milk. Heat to boiling, stirring constantly. Boil and stir for one minute. Mix in turkey, peas and carrots; set aside. Roll out one pie crust and place into a 9"x9" baking pan. Pour turkey mixture into pan. Roll remaining crust into an 11-inch square; cut out vents with a small cookie cutter. Place crust over filling; turn edges under and crimp. Bake at 425 degrees for about 35 minutes, or until golden. Makes 4 to 6 servings.

1  Friday _____

2 Saturday _____

3 Sunday _____ **Daylight Savings Ends**

November

_____ Monday **4**

Election Day _____ Tuesday **5**

_____ Wednesday **6**

_____ Thursday **7**

_____ Friday **8**

_____ Saturday **9**

_____ Sunday **10**

November

11  Monday   **Veterans' Day**
                                                   Remembrance Day (Canada)

12 Tuesday

13 Wednesday

14 Thursday

15 Friday

16 Saturday

17 Sunday

November

Monday 18

Tuesday 19

Wednesday 20

Thursday 21

Friday 22

Saturday 23

Sunday 24

November

25 Monday

26 Tuesday

27 Wednesday   Hanukkah

28 Thursday   Thanksgiving

29 Friday

30 Saturday

December

December

Sunday	Monday	Tuesday
1	2	3
8	9	10
15	16	17
22	23	24
29	30	31 New Year's Eve

November
S	M	T	W	T	F	S
					1	2
3	4	5	6	7	8	9
10	11	12	13	14	15	16
17	18	19	20	21	22	23
24	25	26	27	28	29	30

January
S	M	T	W	T	F	S
			1	2	3	4
5	6	7	8	9	10	11
12	13	14	15	16	17	18
19	20	21	22	23	24	25
26	27	28	29	30	31	

2013

Wednesday	Thursday	Friday	Saturday
4	5	6	7
11	12	13	14
18	19	20	21 **First Day of Winter**
25 **Christmas**	26 **Boxing Day (Canada)**	27	28

At Christmas play and make good cheer,
For Christmas comes but once a year.

— Thomas Tusser

December

Lasagna Florentine

1 lb. ground beef
1/2 c. onion, chopped
2 to 3 cloves garlic, minced
26-oz. jar spaghetti sauce, divided
16-oz. container cottage cheese
10-oz. pkg. frozen spinach, thawed and drained

12-oz. pkg. shredded mozzarella cheese, divided
1/2 c. grated Parmesan cheese, divided
2 eggs, beaten
9 lasagna noodles, cooked

In a skillet over medium heat, brown beef, onion and garlic. Drain; stir in spaghetti sauce and set aside. In a large bowl, combine cottage cheese, spinach, 2 cups mozzarella cheese, 1/4 cup Parmesan cheese and eggs. In an ungreased 13"x9" baking pan, layer one cup sauce mixture, 3 noodles and 1/2 cup cottage cheese mixture; repeat layering once. Top with remaining 3 noodles, sauce mixture, mozzarella and Parmesan. Cover with aluminum foil; bake at 350 degrees for 30 minutes. Uncover; bake for an additional 15 minutes. Let stand for 10 minutes before serving. Makes 9 servings.

December

Monday 2

Tuesday 3

Wednesday 4

Thursday 5

Friday 6

Saturday 7

Sunday 8

December

9 Monday

10 Tuesday

11 Wednesday

12 Thursday

13 Friday

14 Saturday

15 Sunday

December

Monday 16

Tuesday 17

Wednesday 18

Thursday 19

Friday 20

First Day of Winter   Saturday 21

Sunday 22

December

23 Monday

24 Tuesday

25 Wednesday   Christmas

26 Thursday   Boxing Day (Canada)

27 Friday

28 Saturday

29 Sunday

December

New Year's Eve

Make a garland of all the Christmas cards you receive...they'll look festive hung around doorways or windows. Save the cards for next year to make gift tags!

2013

January
S	M	T	W	T	F	S
		1	2	3	4	5
6	7	8	9	10	11	12
13	14	15	16	17	18	19
20	21	22	23	24	25	26
27	28	29	30	31		

February
S	M	T	W	T	F	S
					1	2
3	4	5	6	7	8	9
10	11	12	13	14	15	16
17	18	19	20	21	22	23
24	25	26	27	28		

March
S	M	T	W	T	F	S
					1	2
3	4	5	6	7	8	9
10	11	12	13	14	15	16
17	18	19	20	21	22	23
24	25	26	27	28	29	30
31						

April
S	M	T	W	T	F	S
	1	2	3	4	5	6
7	8	9	10	11	12	13
14	15	16	17	18	19	20
21	22	23	24	25	26	27
28	29	30				

May
S	M	T	W	T	F	S
			1	2	3	4
5	6	7	8	9	10	11
12	13	14	15	16	17	18
19	20	21	22	23	24	25
26	27	28	29	30	31	

June
S	M	T	W	T	F	S
						1
2	3	4	5	6	7	8
9	10	11	12	13	14	15
16	17	18	19	20	21	22
23	24	25	26	27	28	29
30						

July
S	M	T	W	T	F	S
	1	2	3	4	5	6
7	8	9	10	11	12	13
14	15	16	17	18	19	20
21	22	23	24	25	26	27
28	29	30	31			

August
S	M	T	W	T	F	S
				1	2	3
4	5	6	7	8	9	10
11	12	13	14	15	16	17
18	19	20	21	22	23	24
25	26	27	28	29	30	31

September
S	M	T	W	T	F	S
1	2	3	4	5	6	7
8	9	10	11	12	13	14
15	16	17	18	19	20	21
22	23	24	25	26	27	28
29	30					

October
S	M	T	W	T	F	S
		1	2	3	4	5
6	7	8	9	10	11	12
13	14	15	16	17	18	19
20	21	22	23	24	25	26
27	28	29	30	31		

November
S	M	T	W	T	F	S
					1	2
3	4	5	6	7	8	9
10	11	12	13	14	15	16
17	18	19	20	21	22	23
24	25	26	27	28	29	30

December
S	M	T	W	T	F	S
1	2	3	4	5	6	7
8	9	10	11	12	13	14
15	16	17	18	19	20	21
22	23	24	25	26	27	28
29	30	31				

2014

January
S	M	T	W	T	F	S
			1	2	3	4
5	6	7	8	9	10	11
12	13	14	15	16	17	18
19	20	21	22	23	24	25
26	27	28	29	30	31	

February
S	M	T	W	T	F	S
						1
2	3	4	5	6	7	8
9	10	11	12	13	14	15
16	17	18	19	20	21	22
23	24	25	26	27	28	

March
S	M	T	W	T	F	S
						1
2	3	4	5	6	7	8
9	10	11	12	13	14	15
16	17	18	19	20	21	22
23	24	25	26	27	28	29
30	31					

April
S	M	T	W	T	F	S
		1	2	3	4	5
6	7	8	9	10	11	12
13	14	15	16	17	18	19
20	21	22	23	24	25	26
27	28	29	30			

May
S	M	T	W	T	F	S
				1	2	3
4	5	6	7	8	9	10
11	12	13	14	15	16	17
18	19	20	21	22	23	24
25	26	27	28	29	30	31

June
S	M	T	W	T	F	S
1	2	3	4	5	6	7
8	9	10	11	12	13	14
15	16	17	18	19	20	21
22	23	24	25	26	27	28
29	30					

July
S	M	T	W	T	F	S
		1	2	3	4	5
6	7	8	9	10	11	12
13	14	15	16	17	18	19
20	21	22	23	24	25	26
27	28	29	30	31		

August
S	M	T	W	T	F	S
					1	2
3	4	5	6	7	8	9
10	11	12	13	14	15	16
17	18	19	20	21	22	23
24	25	26	27	28	29	30
31						

September
S	M	T	W	T	F	S
	1	2	3	4	5	6
7	8	9	10	11	12	13
14	15	16	17	18	19	20
21	22	23	24	25	26	27
28	29	30				

October
S	M	T	W	T	F	S
			1	2	3	4
5	6	7	8	9	10	11
12	13	14	15	16	17	18
19	20	21	22	23	24	25
26	27	28	29	30	31	

November
S	M	T	W	T	F	S
						1
2	3	4	5	6	7	8
9	10	11	12	13	14	15
16	17	18	19	20	21	22
23	24	25	26	27	28	29
30						

December
S	M	T	W	T	F	S
	1	2	3	4	5	6
7	8	9	10	11	12	13
14	15	16	17	18	19	20
21	22	23	24	25	26	27
28	29	30	31			

Notes

Phone Numbers & Emergency Contacts

Phone Numbers &
Emergency Contacts

Birthdays &
Anniversaries

Birthdays &
Anniversaries

_____

_____

_____

_____

_____

_____

_____

_____

_____

_____

_____

_____

_____

_____

_____

_____

Gift List

Gift / Card